Different cultures have different ways of dying. Old people of the Omaha tribe of Native Americans would stay behind when the rest of their family group moved camp. They were left enough food for just a few days.

Some species of birds live to a great age. Cocky, a male sulphur-crested cockatoo, died in London in 1982 aged over 80.

The most famous hospice in the world was founded by a nun called Mother Teresa. Her hospice was founded to look after people dying on the streets of Calcutta.

Er... I can't think of anything! Err...

Buddhists believe that their dying thoughts will have an important influence on their next life.

Some Hindus try to say the word 'om' with their last breath. They believe that this may help them to escape the cycle of reincarnation.

Trees live a lot longer than animals. The oldest tree is thought to be 'General Sherman', a giant sequoia tree in California about 3,000 years old.

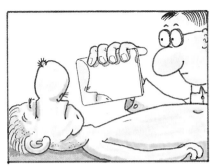

Test for death: Mirror
Breath should cause steam to appear
on a mirror held to the mouth.

Test for death: Pulse
A pulse shows that the
heart is still beating.

Test for death: Light
A modern test for brain stem death is to see
if the pupils of the eye contract in bright light.

Brain
stem

TESTING FOR DEATH

Death doesn't happen to all parts of a body at once. It takes time. For instance, brain cells die four minutes after the heart has stopped beating, but arterial grafts can be made seventy-two hours later. So it's not always easy to know exactly when somebody is dead.

The effects of extreme cold, called hypothermia, and of certain trance-like states such as catalepsy, have often been mistaken for death because breathing and heartbeat couldn't be detected. In fact, in the past, burial alive by mistake may have been quite common.

Nowadays, death is said to have happened when the brain stem stops working. The brain stem sits at the back of the skull. It controls vital body functions such as heartbeat and breathing. Modern instruments can detect breathing and heartbeat very accurately.

Queen Anne Boleyn's head
continued to move its lips
after it had been chopped off.

Around 1308 the philosopher Duns Scotus was buried in a vault in Cologne. When the vault was reopened shortly after, Duns Scotus was found outside his coffin. His hands were torn from trying to open the door of the vault. He had been buried alive.

History Horrors!
Dead!

CONTENTS

FRANKLIN WATTS
LONDON ● SYDNEY

DYING

All living things die. It's the one thing we can all be certain of. In the past, dying was a lot more unpleasant than it is today. The average age of people when they died in the Stone Age was less than eighteen years. The main causes of death were disease and violence.

Fortunately, in western countries nowadays, most people die peacefully in old age. There are even special nursing homes called hospices to care for people who are dying of incurable illnesses.

The image of the Grim Reaper is often associated with death.

On the island of Samoa sick old chiefs used to ask to be buried alive.

The lifespan of the elephant is roughly the same as that of humans - about seventy years.

Some species of mayfly live for only a few hours after they emerge from their larvae.

Test for death: Blood
The Romans would chop off a finger to see if it bled.

Test for Death: Smoke
Some tribes of Native Americans would blow smoke
up the bottom to test for any revival of life.

Test for Death: Nipple Forceps
In the nineteenth century Dr Josat invented
a pair of nipple forceps to test for reaction to
pain. Reaction to pain is also a modern test
for brain stem death.

Many people stay up all night beside
the body of a dead friend or relative.
One reason for this custom is to make
sure that the dead person is really
dead and not just unconscious.

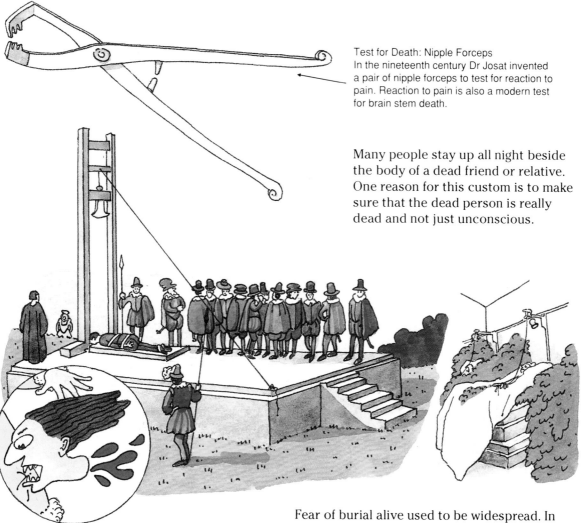

In 1541 the head of a woman guillotined
on the Halifax gibbet flew through the
air and gripped the clothing of a
passerby with its teeth.

Fear of burial alive used to be widespread. In
the Munich Waiting Mortuary, founded in 1791,
corpses were kept for up to seventy-two hours
in a sloping position before burial. Cords were
attached to their fingers in such a way that the
slightest movement would cause bells to ring.

DEAD BODIES

After death the muscles of the body relax. Relaxation starts in the jaw which falls open, and then spreads out through the body. At the same time, because the blood has stopped circulating, it sinks and causes stains on the skin which look like bruises. About six hours later, rigor mortis sets in. This is a stiffening of the muscles which again starts at the jaw and spreads out through the body. Rigor mortis normally lasts about thirty hours, then relaxation of the muscles spreads out once more from the jaw. Rigor mortis may set in immediately if death occurs at a time of stress. This is why suicides may be found gripping the revolver or sword with which they killed themselves.

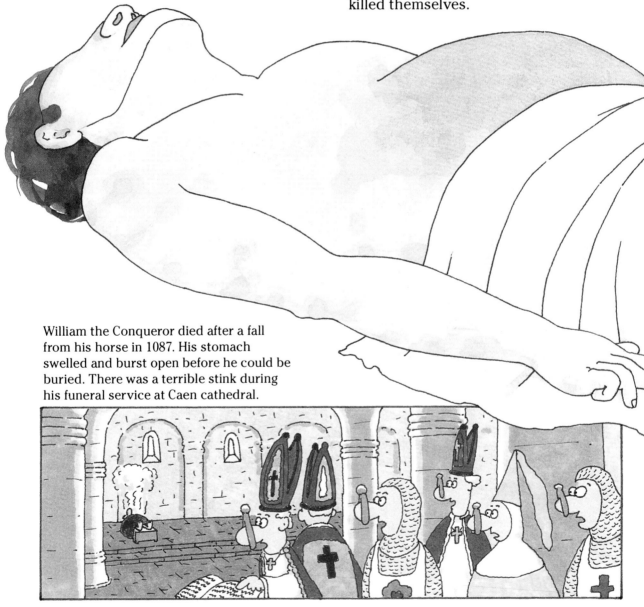

William the Conqueror died after a fall from his horse in 1087. His stomach swelled and burst open before he could be buried. There was a terrible stink during his funeral service at Caen cathedral.

In a warm climate, putrefaction, or rotting, starts after a few days. First, a greenish tinge appears around the stomach and spreads outwards. Then, the stomach swells up with gases like a balloon, and can burst open. Finally, liquefaction (going runny) starts at the eyeballs and finishes with the stomach, liver and womb (in women). Bones do not putrefy.

In subzero temperatures, bodies do not decompose (rot).

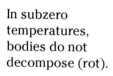

A 45 year old woman died standing upright in a timber yard in the town of Wahncau in Germany. Rigor mortis had set in at the moment of death.

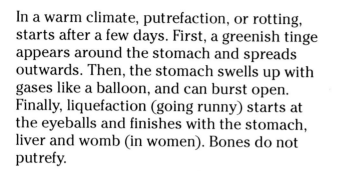

eek!

If death occurs during exercise, rigor mortis can set in immediately. During the charge of the Light Brigade in 1854, an officer's head was blown from his body. The body galloped on upright and stiff in the saddle with his sword still held high.

7

FUNERALS

About two million people die every year in the USA alone, so dealing with dead bodies is a major industry. Normally the first people to handle the dead are nurses and doctors. They tidy the hair and nails, tie up the jaw, put a plug in the bottom and probably they will remove dentures and jewellery. From that point the funeral directors, or undertakers, take over. They take the body away in a temporary coffin and prepare it for burial or cremation. The funeral director's job includes embalming the corpse, supplying the coffin, sending out invitations for the funeral and booking time at a crematorium or buying a plot of land for a burial. In the past, undertakers were often carpenters, because carpenters knew how to make coffins.

The coffin should be the height of the body plus two inches, and it should be the width of the shoulders across. Traditionally, coffins were made of oak or elm; nowadays, they are more likely to be made of veneered chipboard.

The death mask of Samuel Johnson

Death masks often are made by moulding clay around the face of a dead person. When the clay is removed there is a perfect impression of the dead person's face on the inside of it, and it can be used as a mould.

Coffin linings are made of base and side sheets which are attached to the coffin, a loose flap to cover the body and a face cloth to cover the head.

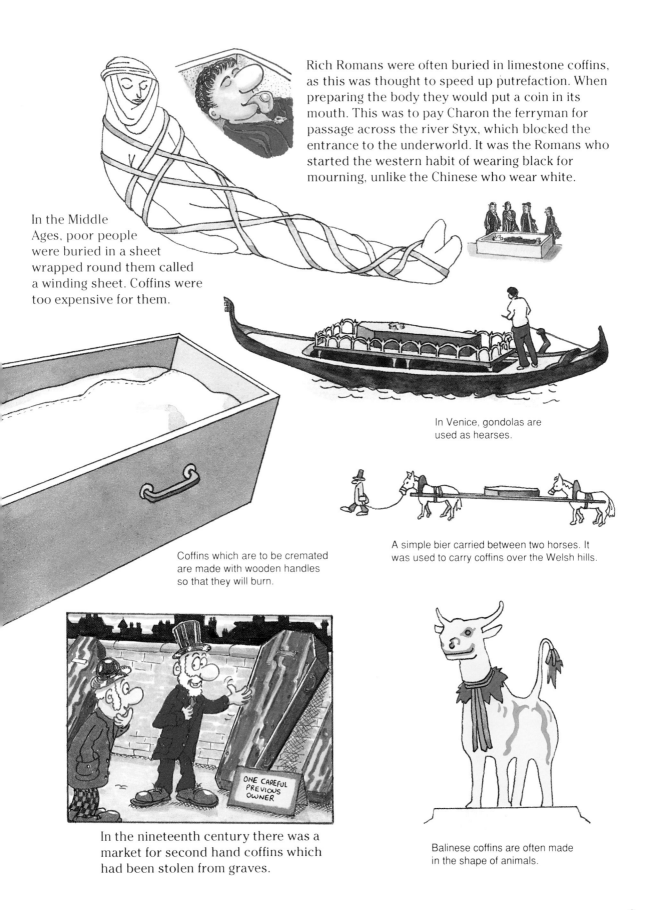

Rich Romans were often buried in limestone coffins, as this was thought to speed up putrefaction. When preparing the body they would put a coin in its mouth. This was to pay Charon the ferryman for passage across the river Styx, which blocked the entrance to the underworld. It was the Romans who started the western habit of wearing black for mourning, unlike the Chinese who wear white.

In the Middle Ages, poor people were buried in a sheet wrapped round them called a winding sheet. Coffins were too expensive for them.

In Venice, gondolas are used as hearses.

Coffins which are to be cremated are made with wooden handles so that they will burn.

A simple bier carried between two horses. It was used to carry coffins over the Welsh hills.

ONE CAREFUL PREVIOUS OWNER

In the nineteenth century there was a market for second hand coffins which had been stolen from graves.

Balinese coffins are often made in the shape of animals.

Home guide to head shrinking

Remove the head from the body.

Make a cut from the back of the neck to the crown of the head.

Remove the skin from the skull and discard the skull.

Sew the eyelids together. Sew the lips together.

EMBALMING

Nowadays many bodies are embalmed. It makes them look peaceful and it stops them smelling before the funeral.

The body is first placed on a trolley and washed in soap and water. Then embalming fluid is pumped into it through an opening in a vein, normally near the armpit. Embalming fluid is a mixture of preservative (usually formaldehyde), disinfectant and colouring. As the fluid spreads through the veins, the body regains a healthy pink colour. Then, after four to six pints have been pumped in, the blood is drained out of the body through another opened vein into a vacuum container on the floor.

The process of replacing the blood with embalming fluid takes about three-quarters of an hour. Afterwards, a surgical instrument called a trocar is plunged into the abdomen and scooped around until all the soft tissue has been removed. Cavity fluid is then pumped in to fill up the empty space.

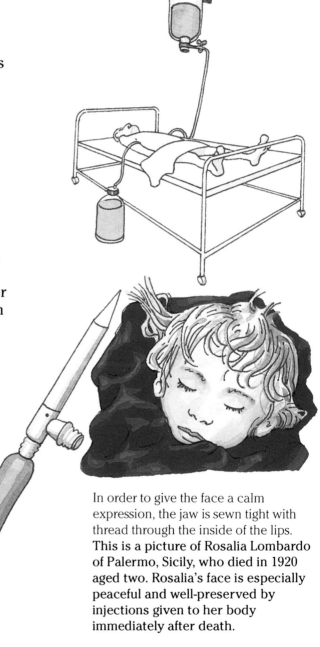

In order to give the face a calm expression, the jaw is sewn tight with thread through the inside of the lips. This is a picture of Rosalia Lombardo of Palermo, Sicily, who died in 1920 aged two. Rosalia's face is especially peaceful and well-preserved by injections given to her body immediately after death.

Boil the scalp and face for two hours.

Place hot stones in the scalp to shrink the skin.

Smoke overnight.

Hang above the fireplace.

Bodies are sometimes embalmed naturally. Tollund Man, who was probably a fertility sacrifice to the goddess Ertha around 500 BC, was preserved intact in a peat bog until discovered in 1950 at Tollund in Denmark. His features are so well-preserved that even the stubble of his beard is completely visible.

Tourists queue to see Lenin's body in his open tomb outside the walls of the Kremlin, Moscow.

A preserved head from ancient Peru. A cactus spine has been inserted through the lips.

Perhaps the most famous body to be embalmed this century is that of Lenin, the leader of the Russian revolution. The body is kept in a temperature-controlled mausoleum in Red Square, Moscow, and is visited by thousands of tourists every year. Every eighteen months the body is taken out and soaked in a special preservative fluid.

In ancient Babylon, bodies were sometimes embalmed in honey. It is said that the body of Alexander the Great was preserved like this.

The Egyptians had several different beliefs about the after-life. Here is one of them:

Ba, the soul, could enter or leave the body at will. It was pictured as a human-headed bird.

After death, Ba made a dangerous journey to the Kingdom of Osiris. A ferryman with eyes in the back of his head took Ba across a river.

Osiris judged new souls at midnight. Ba was then weighed against the feather of virtue. If he had been good, the feather would be heavier.

MUMMIES AND EMBALMING

The ancient Egyptians believed that it was necessary to preserve the body of a dead person in order for that dead person to be reborn. Belief in resurrection after death was centred around the cult of the god Osiris. Osiris was born a man, died, and was mummified by the heavenly doctor Anubis; he was then reborn as a god. The Egyptians believed that by following the same process of mummification, they too could be resurrected. Millions of Egyptians were mummified during the course of the ancient Egyptian civilisation.

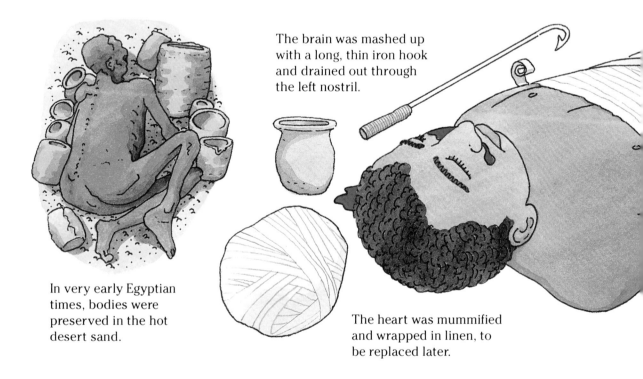

In very early Egyptian times, bodies were preserved in the hot desert sand.

The brain was mashed up with a long, thin iron hook and drained out through the left nostril.

The heart was mummified and wrapped in linen, to be replaced later.

Good souls were given land in the kingdom of Osiris.

Bad souls were roasted in a fire and hacked to pieces.

Anubis was the god of the dead. He had the head of a jackal.

The body was dried out with natron, a kind of soda. Drying took about seventy days. After drying the body was washed and oiled before being wrapped tightly in linen bandages.

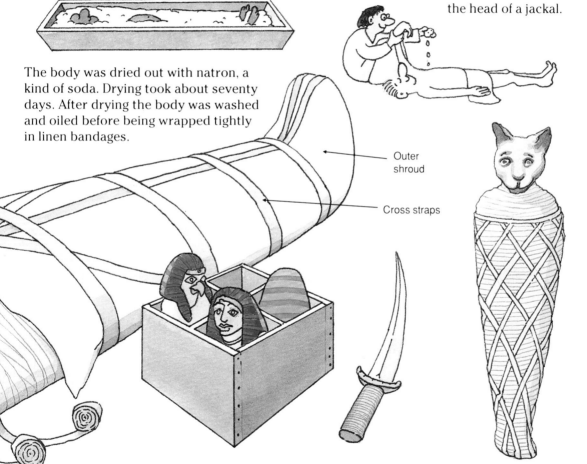

Outer shroud

Cross straps

Intestines and other organs were removed through a cut in the abdomen. The priest would plunge his arm in up to the armpit to reach to the top of the lungs. Internal organs were often kept separately in special pots called canopic jars.

Mummified cats were sacred to Bast, the goddess of pleasure.

BURIAL

If dead bodies are left lying around, they quickly rot and become a danger to health. Throughout history the commonest way to dispose of the dead has been to bury them underground. In some of the earliest graves of prehistoric Europe, stones were often laid on top of a body. It was thought that this would stop the dead from returning to haunt the living. For the same reason the feet were often tied together. Red ochre might be sprinkled on a body to represent the blood and strength it would need in an afterlife.

In modern graves there should be a depth of about six feet between the coffin lid and the surface. At the end of the funeral a few handfuls of earth are scattered on the coffin. The rest of the earth is replaced using a mechanical digger after the mourners have left.

If a body is to be buried at sea, holes must be drilled into the coffin so that water can get in to make the coffin sink.

The Vikings sometimes buried their dead under the thresholds of their houses. This was because they thought that the souls of the dead could defend their houses against evil spirits.

Other ways to dispose of bodies

The Aborigines of Australia left dead bodies in trees.

Hurry up –
He's going off!

In the Solomon Islands the dead were laid out on a reef for the sharks to eat.

Tibetans have no respect for dead bodies once the soul has left them, and will even hack them to pieces for the birds to eat.

In China it is considered very important to bury a corpse in the right spot. An astrological chart with an inset compass is often used to determine the exact position and alignment for the body.

Suicide is a sin in the Christian religion. People who committed suicide were not allowed burial in Christian graveyards and were often buried at crossroads.

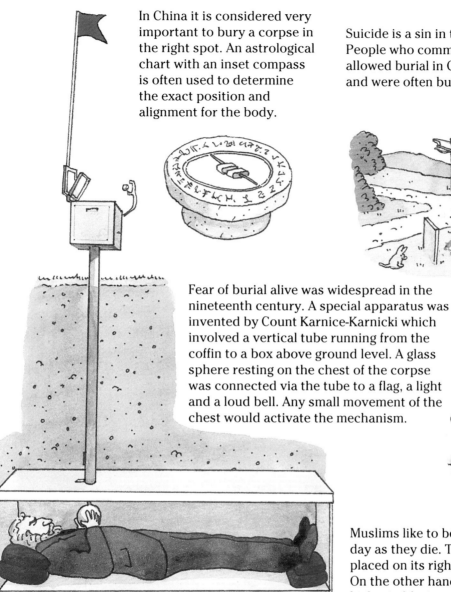

Fear of burial alive was widespread in the nineteenth century. A special apparatus was invented by Count Karnice-Karnicki which involved a vertical tube running from the coffin to a box above ground level. A glass sphere resting on the chest of the corpse was connected via the tube to a flag, a light and a loud bell. Any small movement of the chest would activate the mechanism.

High in the mountains of the Hindu Kush, bodies are buried upright in the snow.

Muslims like to be buried on the same day as they die. The body should be placed on its right side, facing Mecca. On the other hand, Buddhists like to be buried facing north.

Some Inuits cover the corpse with a small igloo. Because of the cold the body will remain for ever unless it is eaten by polar bears.

The Parsees of Bombay used to leave their dead on the top of tall towers to be eaten by vultures. The vultures devour the corpses to the bone within five minutes.

GRAVEYARDS

Cemeteries are places for burial other than churchyards. Cemetery comes from the Greek word *koimeterion* which means 'dormitory'.

Christians were originally buried inside churches, not below ground.

By AD 752, many churches had become ridiculously overcrowded with dead bodies. Arms and legs sometimes stuck out of the floors and walls. So a decree from the Pope allowed graveyards to be added to churches.

However, by the seventeenth century, the same problem of overcrowding was ruining the graveyards. Between 1810 and 1830 in one graveyard in London 14,000 bodies were buried, some only two feet deep. Bones were even dug up and sold to make fertiliser.

By the nineteenth century, the case for cemeteries separate from churchyards became overwhelming. One of the first major cemeteries to be built was the Père Lachaise in Paris.

Forest Lawns Memorial Parks near Los Angeles, America, comprises four cemeteries which cover an area of two square miles. The first, established at Glendale in 1914, is home to the largest religious painting in the USA.

Emperor Constantine

The ancient Greeks and Romans used to bury their dead outside their cities. But during the Roman Empire the fashion grew for burial in underground chambers, called catacombs, within the city of Rome.

Early Christians dug catacombs beneath the church of St. Peter, the first Pope, so that they could be buried near to Peter's body. From there it was a small step to burial inside the church. The first person to be buried inside a church was the Emperor Constantine in AD 337.

In the nineteenth century, Mr Wilson of London planned to build a pyramid which would have been bigger than that of Cheops, big enough to house five million bodies. Wilson's pyramid would have been the largest cemetery ever built, but it was never completed.

As churches became more crowded, bodies were sometimes removed from graves and placed in charnel houses.

There are thousands of bones in the charnel house of the Capuchin Church of the Immaculate Conception in Rome, arranged in complicated designs on the ceilings and walls.

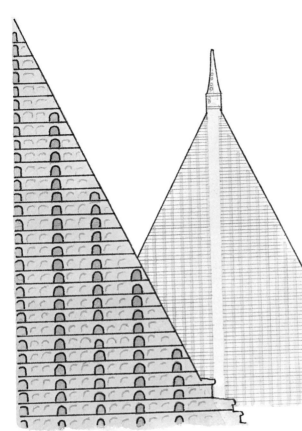

Zey say people are dying to get in zere!

To increase the popularity of the Père Lachaise cemetery, its owners dug up the bodies of famous people and reburied them there. Among the famous people reburied in this way were the playwrights Molière and Beaumarchais.

At the charnel house of the Capuchin Monastery in Palermo, Sicily, the bodies were first dried and are preserved fully clothed.

The Brookwood cemetery near Woking in Southern England was opened in 1854. A special railway, called the Brookwood Necropolis Railway, was built to carry coffins from London, sixty miles away.

The Taj Mahal is one of the seven wonders of the modern world. It was built by the Mogul Emperor Shah-Jehan for his favourite wife Arjamund Begum. Arjamund died in 1631. Work on the mausoleum started in 1632.

MEMORIALS

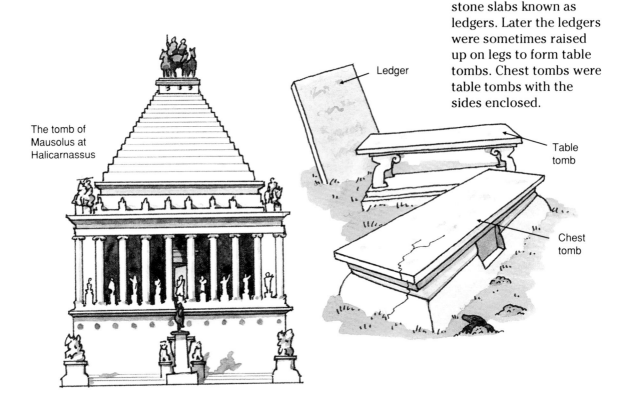

The tomb of Mausolus at Halicarnassus

Ledger

Table tomb

Chest tomb

The earliest Christian tombstones were simple stone slabs known as ledgers. Later the ledgers were sometimes raised up on legs to form table tombs. Chest tombs were table tombs with the sides enclosed.

It is human vanity to hope that we shall be remembered after we die. In many historic cultures, more money has been spent on memorials for the dead than on homes for the living. The richer and more powerful the dead person, the bigger the memorial. Mausolus was a Persian King in what is now south-western Turkey. His huge, white marble tomb at Halicarnassus was one of the Seven Wonders of the Ancient World. It was built by his wife Artemisia (who was also his sister). Artemisia mixed his ashes in wine and drank the mixture. She later joined him in their mausoleum.

It took 20,000 men working for 22 years to build the Taj Mahal.

The Emperor wanted his building to be unique. When it was finished, the hands of the craftsmen were chopped off so that they couldn't build another one like it.

Elvis Presley is buried at his home called Gracelands, in Memphis, USA, which is now an Elvis museum as well as his mausoleum.

The burial mounds of native North American Indians were sometimes built in the shapes of birds and animals. Some of these mounds were built as early as 700 BC.

Great Serpent Mound, Ohio

The tomb built for the Chinese Emperor Qin Shihuangdi was said to contain rivers of mercury. Crossbows were set to fire at grave robbers automatically. The workmen who built the tomb were walled up inside to stop them giving away the secrets of its construction.

The great pyramids are among the largest structures ever built. The pyramid of Cheops is made up of 2,500,000 blocks of stone of an average weight of 2.5 tonnes. Its height is over 140 metres and 100,000 workers took more than 20 years to build it.

The tomb of Karl Marx, the founder of communism, is in Highgate Cemetery in London.

GRAVE ROBBERS

Nowadays, to help science, many people give their bodies for medical research. Enough bodies are given each year for the researchers and medical students who need them. It wasn't always so easy. For many years, Christians believed that at the end of the world their physical bodies would be resurrected. If bodies were cut up by researchers, resurrection would be impossible.

Post-mortems were carried out by Christians in Byzantium as early as AD 50. In Parma in 1286, bodies were cut open to try to discover the cause of the plague. These were exceptions. Even as late as 1380, Pope Boniface banned the boiling or cutting up of corpses. It was only during the Renaissance that dissection was permitted in Europe. Even then, it was only allowed on the bodies of executed criminals.

There was always a shortage of bodies. And the shortage grew worse with the growth of medical schools in the eighteenth century. Medical students needed bodies to practise on. Grave robbers, or resurrectionists, stepped in to supply the bodies.

Grave robbing made easy

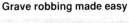

Dig a vertical shaft to the head of the coffin.

Cover with sacking to reduce the noise.

Prise off the coffin lid.

Haul out the body using a noose tied round the neck.

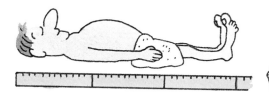

Children's bodies were often sold by the foot: six shillings for the first foot and nine pence per inch thereafter.

The Crouch gang was one of the most famous gangs of grave robbers. They operated in London in the early 1800s.

This picture is taken from *The Resurrectionists* by the cartoonist Thomas Rowlandson (1756-1827).

William Harvey, who discovered that blood circulates round the body, dissected the dead bodies of his own father and sister.

In the sixteenth century, the French government gave one criminal per year to the medical profession for live dissection. Live dissection was also practised by Greek doctors in ancient Alexandria.

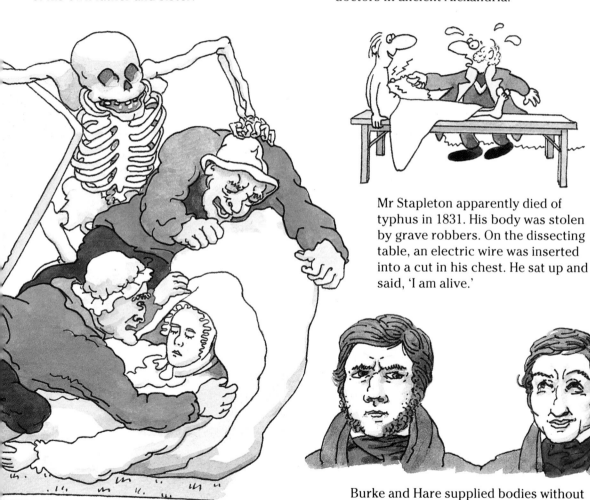

Mr Stapleton apparently died of typhus in 1831. His body was stolen by grave robbers. On the dissecting table, an electric wire was inserted into a cut in his chest. He sat up and said, 'I am alive.'

Burke and Hare supplied bodies without robbing graves. They just killed their victims. It was less effort. Burke was executed in Edinburgh in 1828. His body was dissected. Hare turned informer and was pardoned. His skeleton can be seen in the anatomy museum at Edinburgh University.

GRAVE GOODS

The custom of burying things with the dead is at least 60,000 years old. The rich and powerful were buried with treasure, and even with their servants. Ordinary people were buried with food and drink and sometimes cups and tools. Things may have been buried with dead bodies because it was believed that they would be useful in the after-life. Much of what we know about ancient people has been learned from studying their grave goods.

The tomb of the Qin Emperor of China contained an army of life-sized clay soldiers and the bodies of all his concubines who were killed specially for his burial.

Some Bronze Age people only buried a dead person's skull with a few possessions.

In ancient China, jaw bones of pigs were buried with the dead.

The Egyptian pyramids were like palaces stuffed with treasures. The tomb of Tutankhamun contained the largest hoard of ancient golden artefacts ever found.

Neanderthal graves 60,000 years old have been found containing the remains of flowers.

The Egyptian queen Her-Neith was buried with her favourite dog.

A thirteenth century Maharajah of Jaipur was buried with his favourite elephant.

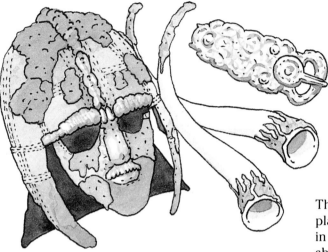

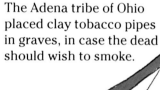

In India, a Mogul prince was buried with his barber.

The burial ship of a Saxon king dating from AD 650 was found at Sutton Hoo. It contained some of the richest treasures ever found in England.

The Adena tribe of Ohio placed clay tobacco pipes in graves, in case the dead should wish to smoke.

In the Middle Ages, consecrated bread was buried in the grave, so that the dead could offer it to God. Priests were buried with a cross and a cup as well as the bread.

The royal tombs of ancient Sumeria had running water so that the dead could drink.

Nowadays, if children die, their favourite toys may be buried with them.

Among other things, the ancient Celts would put games in the grave so that the dead would have something to amuse themselves with in the next world.

RELICS

The remains of bodies often have been thought to have magical powers.

The cannibals of Melanesia used to eat the bodies of their enemies, not for the meat, but in order to aquire the strength of their victims. They said the meat tasted of pork. They called the flesh of missionaries 'long pig'.

The bones of Christian saints are still thought by many to have miraculous powers, and pilgrims travel long distances to see them. Arm, leg and head bones are considered the most holy. In the Middle Ages, these holy relics were big business. Pilgrims had money to spend, just like tourists today. Bones were often divided up. John the Baptist's went to Amiens, Rhodes, Besançon and several other places. Today such beliefs are less common.

St Hugh of Lincoln bit off two pieces of Mary Magdelene's arm bone when on a pilgrimage to Normandy, and smuggled them back to England.

A Buddhist ritual trumpet made from a human thigh bone.

Food facts

Leave a toe for me!

Not only the Melanesians ate human flesh. Some aboriginal Australian tribes ate the flesh of dead relatives as a mark of respect.

Dinner's nearly ready!

In some parts of Indonesia the liquids of a decomposing body were mixed with rice and eaten. It was believed that this food had magical properties.

Careful with Grandad's head son!

On some islands of Melanesia the skull of the deceased is given to a near relative to use as a drinking cup.

One of the vertebrae of the astronomer Galileo was stolen in 1757. It is now displayed in Padua.

One of the holiest shrines of Buddhism is the Temple of the Tooth at Kandy in Sri Lanka, where Buddha's left canine tooth is kept.

The ancient Celts hung the heads of their enemies from their horses and outside their houses.

A hair from the beard of the Prophet Mohammed is preserved in resin in the Topkapi museum in Istanbul.

Frederich Ruysh (1638-1731) made tableaux from the skeletons of children together with preserved parts of the human body and stuffed birds. His collection was bought by Peter the Great of Russia.

CREMATION

In AD 789, Emperor Charlemagne decreed death for anyone practising cremation. Cremation was considered unchristian because it was thought that a burned body could not be resurrected at the Last Judgement.

The first cremations in the USA were carried out in Washington in 1876, in the private crematorium of a doctor, Julius Lemogne. In Britain, the first legal cremation took place in 1883 when Dr William Price, an 83 year old Welsh druidic priest, cremated his five month old baby, whom he had named Jesus Christ Price.

Modern crematoriums reduce a body to ashes in about one and a half hours. The newest models working at temperatures up to 1,200 degrees centigrade are even quicker. Wood ash from the coffin is light, and goes up the chimney together with any water vapour, leaving the bones and the ashes of the body behind. Any metal, for instance gold from teeth, is collected from the ashes. Finally, the bone fragments are crushed to a fine powder in a special machine. The final residue per adult weighs about three kilograms. This is collected into a tin can with a screw top, ready to be emptied into an urn or to be scattered.

An early crematorium

The Beaker people who lived in Europe around 4,000 years ago used to collect the ashes of their dead in beakers or decorated pots.

Suttee was a cruel tradition common in India until banned by the British in 1829. Widows were expected to burn alive with their dead husbands, sometimes cradling their husband's head on their laps and lighting the fire themselves. In 1780, when Rajah Ajit Singh was cremated, sixty-four of his wives were burned alive with him.

Gypsy kings and queens are burned in their caravans.

Os resectum is a mixture of burial and cremation. A finger is cut off and buried, while the rest of the body is burned. The buried finger is the seed for the new body which will be resurrected on judgement day.

Viking leaders were placed in their favourite long boat, which was then set alight and pushed out to sea.

The poet Percy Bysshe Shelley drowned off the coast of Italy in 1822. His body was burned on an open fire on the beach. Wine, incense and oil were thrown on to the flames. Trelawney, his friend, plucked the heart from the fire, badly burning his own hand. The heart was returned to England in a box.

Nowadays, cremation is forbidden for orthodox Jews, Parsees, Muslims and Greek Orthodox Christians. Hindus always cremate their dead. The eldest son lights the funeral pyre.

LIFE AFTER DEATH

Most people throughout history have believed that their spirit continues to live after their mortal body is dead, although there has always been a minority of atheists who do not believe in God and think that when you're dead you're dead.

The ancient Mesopotamians believed that the souls of the dead fell into a huge pit called the 'Land of No Return'.

The Vikings believed that the souls of warriors who died in battle went to a life of feasting in Valhalla, the hall of the god Odin.

Christians believe that the good go to Heaven and the bad go to Hell. However, there may be a long time to wait until Judgement Day. Because Hell is such a severe punishment, most Christians believe that the dead go to be purified before being admitted to heaven. This stage of purification is called purgatory and can be thought of as a temporary hell.

The ancient Celts believed that the afterworld was a place of happiness where they could indulge in all their favourite activities. There would be lots to eat and drink and plenty of fighting, and wounds would heal overnight. For this reason the Celts did not fear death and often went into battle naked.

I tell you these are not just beans - they are human beans!

Rubbish!

Pull the other one.

Who do you want to be when you grow up?

Pythagoras

Pythagoras, the ancient Greek philosopher, believed that broad beans contained the souls of the dead so he forbade his followers to eat them.

Hindus and Buddhists believe that the soul experiences many lives. After death the soul is reborn in a new young body which can be an animal or a person. This is called reincarnation. Eventually very good, wise people can escape the cycle of reincarnation and enter into a state of one-ness with the universe called nirvana.

The Aborigines believe that their spirits exist before and after life in a state called Dreamtime. The spirits of the tribe and of its special animals are reborn again and again.

Muslims believe that the souls of warriors who die in a Jihad, or holy war, will go straight to heaven.

The Greek underworld was a grey place of shadows called the Kingdom of Hades. Dead people were pale shadows of their former selves. Hades was guarded by a giant three-headed dog called Cerberus and surrounded by the river Styx. A corner of Hades called Elysium was slightly more pleasant and was reserved for heroes.

Cryonics is a method of freeze drying bodies in the hope that they can be thawed out and brought back to life in the future. People ask for this treatment because they believe that a cure for the cause of their death may be discovered in the future.

After death the body must be connected immediately to a heart-lung machine and packed in water ice.

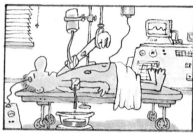

Later the blood is drained out of the body, and replaced with preservative fluid.

DEEP FROZEN FUTURE

The population of the world is now 5,000 million people and it's still growing. About 5 million tonnes of dead bodies have to be disposed of every year. The problems of disposal are going to increase in the future.

Cryonics poses many problems. In particular, would future generations want to revive thousands of frozen bodies?

Millions of bodies were mummified in ancient Egypt. If it were possible for us to revive them, would we want all those ancient Egyptians to look after?

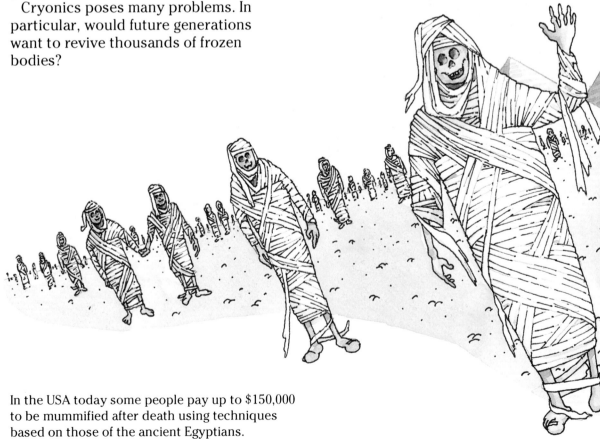

In the USA today some people pay up to $150,000 to be mummified after death using techniques based on those of the ancient Egyptians.

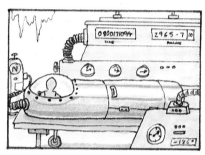

Finally the body is frozen in liquid nitrogen. Keeping it frozen is very expensive.

It's unlikely that cryonics is effective. To really work, bodies should be frozen before they die.

Are you dead yet?

Nearly!

The first dead body to be permanently frozen was James Bedford, a Californian teacher of psychology, in 1967.

Quick drying may be used in future to preserve bodies for later revival. In 1954 the body of a ten year old Inca prince was discovered in a cave on a mountain near Santiago, Chile. The child had died 500 years before but the body had been very well preserved in the cold, dry air.

The frozen bodies of mammoths have been found in the ice of Siberia. Their meat could still be eaten after thousands of years. In the future people may consider it wasteful to burn or bury 5 million tonnes of nutritious dead bodies every year. They could be frozen and eaten instead!

INDEX

This edition 2005
Franklin Watts
96 Leonard Street
London EC2A 4XD

Franklin Watts Australia
45-51 Huntley Street
Alexandria NSW 2015

Originally published as
Horrible Histories: Dead!

© 1993 Lazy Summer Books Ltd
Illustrated by Lazy Summer Books Ltd

ISBN 0 7496 6200 X

A CIP catalogue record for
this book is available from
the British Library.

Printed in Hong Kong